BEING DEAF

UNIT 1
PERSPECTIVES ON DEAFNESS: AN INTRODUCTION
PREPARED FOR THE COURSE TEAM BY
GEORGE TAYLOR AND SUSAN GREGORY

PAINTING ON COVER AND TITLE PAGE BY TREVOR LANDELL

 The Open University

THIS COURSE HAS BEEN PRODUCED WITH FUNDING
FROM THE DEPARTMENT OF HEALTH

D251 Core Course Team

ANNE DARBY Diploma Placements Officer, Faculty of Social Sciences

SUSAN GREGORY Senior Lecturer in Psychology, Faculty of Social Sciences (Course Team Chair)

YVONNE HOLMES Secretary, Faculty of Social Sciences

LINDA JANES Course Manager, Faculty of Social Sciences

GEORGE TAYLOR Lecturer in Interdisciplinary Social Sciences, Faculty of Social Sciences

Other Open University Contributors

JULIET BISHOP Research Fellow in Social Sciences, Faculty of Social Sciences

DEBBIE CROUCH Designer

TIM DANT Research Fellow in Health and Social Welfare, Continuing Education

VIC FINKELSTEIN Senior Lecturer in Health and Social Welfare, Continuing Education

GERALD HALES Research Fellow, Institute of Educational Technology

FIONA HARRIS Editor

KEITH HOWARD Graphic Artist

MARY JOHN Senior Lecturer in Psychology, Faculty of Social Sciences

VIC LOCKWOOD BBC Producer

KEN PATTON BBC Producer

ALISON TUCKER BBC Producer

External Consultants

LORNA ALLSOP Centre for Deaf Studies, University of Bristol

LARAINE CALLOW Consultant in Deafness

MARY FIELDER National Council of Social Workers with Deaf People

GILLIAN M. HARTLEY Teacher, Thorn Park School, Bradford

LYNNE HAWCROFT Royal National Institute for the Deaf

JIM KYLE Centre for Deaf Studies, University of Bristol

PADDY LADD London Deaf Video Project

CARLO LAURENZI National Deaf Children's Society

CLIVE MASON Presenter, BBC 'See Hear'

RUKHSANA MEHERALI Educational Psychologist, Royal School for the Deaf, Derby

DOROTHY MILES Writer, Lecturer and Poet

BOB PECKFORD British Deaf Association

CHRISTINE PLAYER Tutor Adviser

SHARON RIDGEWAY National Council of Social Workers with Deaf People

JANICE SILO Teacher of the Deaf, Derbyshire

External Assessors

MARY BRENNAN Co-director, MA and Advanced Diploma in Sign Language Studies, University of Durham

MALCOLM PAYNE Head of Department of Applied Community Studies, Manchester Polytechnic

Sign Language Interpreters

BYRON CAMPBELL

ELIZABETH JONES

KYRA POLLITT

LINDA RICHARDS

The Open University
Walton Hall, Milton Keynes
MK7 6AB

First published 1991

Designed by the Graphic Design Group of the Open University

Printed in the United Kingdom by The Open University

ISBN 0 7492 0047 2

This publication forms part of the Open University course D251 Issues in Deafness. If you have not enrolled on the course and would like to buy this or other Open University material, please write to Open University Educational Enterprises Ltd, 12 Cofferidge Close, Stony Stratford, Milton Keynes MK11 1BY, United Kingdom. If you wish to enquire about enrolling as an Open University student, please write to the Admissions Office, The Open University, P.O. Box 48, Walton Hall, Milton Keynes MK7 6AB, United Kingdom.

Unit 1 Perspectives on Deafness: An Introduction

prepared for the course team by George Taylor and Susan Gregory

Contents

Associated study materials

Video One, *Sandra's Story: The History of a Deaf Family*

Reader One, Article 1, 'Janet's Diary', Janet Goodwill.

Reader One, Article 6, 'The Chance to Speak for Ourselves', Heather MacDonald.

Reader One, Article 7, 'Deafness: The Treatment', Lorraine Fletcher.

Reader One, Article 9, 'School Experiences', Clive Mason.

Reader One, Article 11, 'Life at Secondary School', Elizabeth Craddock.

Reader One, Article 13, 'Education for Life?', Christopher Reid.

Reader One, Article 14, 'Training to Teach', Sarah Elsey.

continued

D251 Issues in Deafness

Aims

The specific aims of this unit are:

1   To examine the notion of deafness and to clarify how the term is used in the course as a whole.
2   To provide a basic introduction to Deaf people, their language, community and culture, through personal accounts and through video.
3   To encourage exploration of personal attitudes to deafness and deaf people.
4   To look at changing ideas about deafness and the changing attitudes to deaf people throughout history.
5   To examine popular understandings of deafness and deaf people.
6   To introduce some of the issues and themes discussed throughout the course, namely:

(a) the Deaf community and who belongs to it;

(b) the contrasting notions of deaf people as disabled and Deaf people as constituting a linguistic and cultural minority group;

(c) the implications of audiological definitions of deafness (deaf) and cultural definitions of deafness (Deaf);

(d) the language of Deaf people and the status of minority group languages;

(e) language and power;

(f) the different constructions of deafness and their different implications.

Beyond these specific aims, the unit has a more general role which is to provide an introduction to the teaching procedures used in the course as a whole and to ways in which you might approach your study of it. Within the course units, for example, different strategies, such as activities and ITQs (In Text Questions), are used; you will also be asked to read from Readers One and Two and from the Set Books, and to watch the four videos which accompany the course. We hope to illustrate through this first unit how these various elements form an integral part of the study of an Open University course. This unit should therefore be studied in conjunction with both the *Study Skills and Resource Booklet* and the *Course Guide* which provide further information about study with the Open University generally and about this course in particular.

Study guide

Week one
Before doing anything else, you should look at Video One, *Sandra's Story*. The course has been designed so that your first introduction to Deaf people, their language, community and culture is through the medium of video rather than print, as this was felt to be more appropriate. **You should look at the video now.**

After looking at the video you should spend week one on Section 1 'Sandra's story' and Section 2 'Attitudes to deafness' in this unit.

Several activities and readings are suggested, and you should do or read these as they arise. It may be tempting to go quickly through some of the attitude scales, but it is felt by the course team that you will get more from the course if you spend some time on these items.

Also, during week one you should skim through the *Study Skills and Resource Booklet* to familiarize yourself with the contents. You should not try to read it all thoroughly at this time. You will need to consult it during the course, and particularly while studying Unit 1, especially if you are a new student of The Open University. At this stage you may find Section 3.4 on using the Readers particularly useful. Many of the Reader articles are referred to several times throughout the course, and keeping good notes as you read will be useful for future reference.

Week two
In week two you should study Section 3 'Who are Deaf people?' and Section 4 'Changing attitudes to deafness'.

Again, you should complete the activities and readings as you encounter them. If you have time to spare during this week, you may like to read more of the articles in Reader One. Each presents a different perspective on 'Being Deaf', and familiarity with a range of the articles will be good background for the course.

Week three
In week three you should study Section 5 'Popular conceptions of deafness' and Section 6 'Conclusion', together with the recommended readings and activities.

For this unit, and for all other units, you should allow yourself time at the end of the three study weeks to review the unit as a whole, to make notes on the basic themes and concepts of the unit, and to review the aims of the unit in order to ensure that you are aware of the main points.

1 Sandra's story

We would like you to start the course by watching Video One. Watch it just as you would a television documentary, making a mental note only of how watching the video makes you feel.

Why start with a video?

The world of Deaf people is a visual world, and many essential elements of Deaf culture and language can only be fully explained and appreciated by presenting them visually. One of the aims of the course is to challenge many of the views that are held of Deaf people and thus it is important that this is reflected in the structure of the course.

Why start with this particular video?

Because it is a dramatic and effective way of introducing you to many of the issues which will be addressed throughout the course. In particular, we want to introduce you to:

Δ   The Deaf community with its own culture and language.

Δ   The visual–spatial communication mode of Deaf people.

Δ   Deaf people relaxed amongst other Deaf people, at home and in the Deaf club.

Δ   The history of one Deaf family.

(You may find it useful to consult Section 3.8 on using video in the *Study Skills and Resource Booklet*.)

1.1 Introducing the family

There have been Deaf people in Sandra Smith's family for six generations, and the video describes how Sandra traced her ancestors back to the village of Bisley where Thomas Smith was born in 1824. Whilst this is of some significance to the Smith family, why should it be of more than a passing interest to you on this course? There are three reasons. First, this family is an example of how the culture and language of the Deaf community has been passed on uninterrupted from one generation to the next. This is unusual, as the vast majority of deaf children are born to hearing parents, and very few Deaf people live in a Deaf family. Second, the history of this family is accessible to us, not only through photographs and local records, but also through the testimony of family members who are able to talk about previous generations. And third, this video raises a number of important issues for the Deaf community which will be recurring themes throughout this course.

ITQ

What do you consider are the important issues for the Deaf community raised in Video One? Make some brief notes now before reading on. Section 3.7 on making notes in the *Study Skills and Resource Booklet* contains useful guidance, which may be helpful here.

◀ Comment
You may wish to watch Video One again, this time making notes as you watch. Do not worry about being too precise or clear on the notes you make. The object of the exercise at this stage of the course is to help you to begin to interact with the course material, so that you can use the material to identify issues. ◀

Video One will be referred to a number of times throughout the course for different purposes. At this point we will draw out some of the major themes in the video to be addressed at different stages of the course. We have divided these themes into four main areas, although they are actually quite closely interlinked:

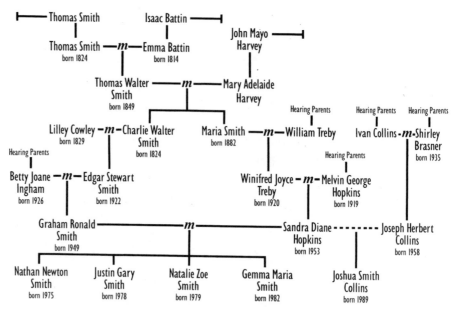

Figure 1.1   Sandra Smith's family tree

Figure 1.2   Wedding photograph from Sandra's archives. Thirteen of those shown are Deaf
(Source: courtesy of Sandra Smith)

Figure 1.3   The Smith family

Figure 1.4   Sandra Smith

Figure 1.5   Nathan Smith

Figure 1.6   Justin Smith

Figure 1.7   Natalie Smith

Figure 1.8   Gemma Smith

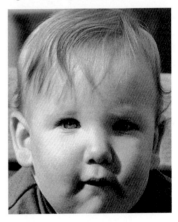

Figure 1.9   Joshua Smith
Collins

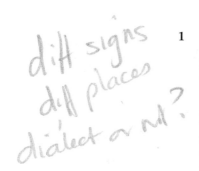

diff signs
diff places
dialect or nd?

1   **Deaf language:** The language used by Sandra Smith and her family is British Sign Language (BSL), the preferred language of the British Deaf community. (BSL is discussed in detail in Unit 3.) You will observe that the communication between the different members of the Smith family flows in much the same way as it does amongst groups of people using speech and not sign language. The children chat to each other about their schooldays. Even whilst Sandra is feeding Joshua with a bottle, she is able to continue her conversation with Gemma. And, in the Deaf club, Sandra and her friends are discussing, in BSL, the San Francisco earthquake of 1989, which happened the day before filming took place.

It would appear to be obvious, therefore, that BSL is an effective means of communication. This is an area of some debate, however, and Deaf people maintain that they are engaged in a continual struggle in defence of their language.

2   **Deaf culture:** Sandra refers to the Deaf club as the place where Deaf people can relax and meet their friends. It also serves another function in Deaf community life: the maintenance of Deaf culture. (Deaf culture is discussed in Unit 2.) Because Deaf people live their lives mostly amongst hearing people, the Deaf club becomes the primary focus of the Deaf community, a place where cultural norms are negotiated and authenticated. (Deaf art as a cultural expression will be discussed in Unit 10. Those Deaf people who do not regularly attend Deaf clubs will be the focus of Unit 4.)

The existence of Deaf culture is the subject of much debate. In Video One, Sandra describes some of the features of Deaf culture, and throughout this course you will encounter references to the culture of the Deaf community and to Deaf people as a cultural and linguistic minority group. In contrast to this perspective on the Deaf community, however, there is a competing view which considers Deaf people as 'disabled', and not as a minority group at all. (This position will be explored in relation to mental health in Unit 6. Unit 9 will explore the political 'common ground' between disabled people and the Deaf community.)

3   **Education:** In Video One Sandra described how her local school for the deaf once again allows sign language to be used for teaching purposes, and encourages the employment of deaf adults to work with deaf children in the classroom. She identifies the Milan Congress of 1880 as the watershed for the education of deaf children. Following this, the second international congress on the education of deaf children, schools for the deaf increasingly adopted oralist teaching methods, and banned the use of sign language within the educational setting. The situation in Britain, as we write, is that formal training for teachers of the deaf does not include sign language training as a compulsory element. Even though a number of schools for the deaf are incorporating sign language into parts of their curricula, education for deaf children is very largely English based and there are very few deaf teachers of the deaf. ('Education and Deaf People' is the title and subject of Unit 5.)

4   **The interface between the deaf world and the hearing world:** Deaf people come into contact with hearing people in all areas of their lives: at work, a visit to the doctor's surgery, shopping, in the mosque and on holiday. Deaf people are accustomed to contact with a wide range of people who have little or no knowledge of the Deaf community and

find communication with deaf people difficult. Specialist facilities for deaf people, whether in the voluntary or the statutory sector, are mostly controlled by hearing people. Formal activities such as a claim for Social Security benefits, or an interview with a solicitor, will usually require the services of an interpreter. And if a deaf person wants advice or counselling of a personal and intimate nature there is usually no one they can turn to other than their local Social Worker with Deaf People (if one exists in their area). Deaf people, like hearing people, often turn to their families and sometimes deaf people ask family members or friends to assist them in these situations, but this is not always appropriate or convenient.

Neighbours - don't know them
education - decision
hosp - comms over baby's hearing.

ITQ

How are hearing people represented in Video One? Sandra Smith makes some specific references to hearing people and the implications of this 'contact' for her family. Pick out some occasions from Video One when Sandra talks about hearing people, and write down those issues that you consider are raised.

We have selected three occasions when a number of important issues are raised about the contact between deaf people and hearing people. First, and most obvious, we learnt that Joshua, Sandra's youngest child, is hearing. Her reaction was one of shock. She had been certain that Joshua was deaf like her other children, and is somewhat disorientated by the news that he is not. It is significant that Sandra does not view this as particularly 'good news'. To be deaf in Sandra's family is the norm, and her sense of identity as a Deaf person has grown from the fact that she has so many Deaf ancestors. Some deaf people say that the birth of a deaf child is a gift to the Deaf community and should be celebrated. How then, would a hearing child born into a Deaf family be greeted? *problems ahead - outside.*

Second, Sandra refers to her neighbours. And, despite the fact that the family has lived in that street for some time, there is little contact and Sandra suspects that their perceptions of deaf people would be inaccurate.

Love hurts
deaf son - same as dhers - with speech

◀ Activity 1
Our 'knowledge' of other people, other groups in society, is the result of a number of influences: family, friends, television, newspapers etc. In your family, or amongst your friends, are deaf people talked about? If so, what kind of things are said about them? Also, in what ways do newspapers and television companies represent deaf people? You may find it useful to make some notes here. ◀

◀ Comment
Later in this unit we will be looking at representations of deaf people in the press. Issues of stereotyping and social categorization will be looked at in Unit 6 and the 'social construction of deafness' is the subject of Unit 8. ◀

Third, Sandra tells Gemma the story of the 'cockerel'. Many families have stories about their ancestors, they act as a sort of 'glue' that binds the different generations together. What is significant in this story is that it describes the point at which a hearing family started to become a Deaf family, and that, whilst the Smith family of today have a very positive view of Deaf people, their ancestors who slew the cockerel considered the birth of the first deaf child to be a punishment. It is like being presented with only the first and last chapters of a book: we know how it started and how it ends, but we do not know how or why it changed in between. Was the changing attitude down the generations of Sandra Smith's family inevitable as more deaf children were born into the family? Is it possible for relationships between Deaf people and hearing people to be based on mutual understanding? And if so, what are the circumstances necessary for this to occur? (Units 5, 6 and 7 focus specifically on the relationship between deaf people and hearing professionals.)

2 Attitudes to deafness

2.1 Self-rating and attitudes

◄ Activity 2

We would like you to pause for a moment now. You have watched Video One, and the central themes in the course have been identified. Before you continue with the course it is important that you explore your own attitudes towards deaf people and to this end we have prepared an exercise. The idea of this exercise is that you rate yourself in terms of your knowledge and awareness in relation to deaf people and the Deaf community. The impact of this exercise will be different for hearing students than it is for deaf students. You may want to consider the implications of this difference.

A good way of doing this is by using a simple straight line scale numbered from 0 to 10:

0   1   2   3   4   5   6   7   8   9   10

Start by estimating your level of knowledge of deaf people. 0 means never having met a deaf person, read a book or an article about deaf people, or had a conversation from which you gained some information. 10 means you have a comprehensive and in-depth knowledge of deaf people. The in-between parts on the scale can be used in a variety of ways. It could mean you have personal knowledge of deaf people, but have never reflected upon this, or you have professional knowledge of deaf issues, but little personal contact with deaf people. You will need to decide for yourself how to assess your own understanding. Place today's date at the point on the scale which you think most closely approximates with your level of knowledge.

Estimating your level of awareness is slightly more difficult. Think of it as the interaction between your intelligence and your feelings. For example, after watching Video One you should realize that Deaf people can express themselves articulately in sign language. If you also now appreciate that deaf people face many obstacles in a society constructed to meet the needs of hearing people and not deaf people, your level of awareness is increased by your capacity to understand and empathize. Mark the scale accordingly. ◄

2.2 Perceptions of deaf people

 ◀ Activity 3
We will ask you to return to the self-rating scale later in the unit. The following exercise is designed to be an exploration into your knowledge base of deaf people and the Deaf community. Here are a number of statements about deaf people: state whether you agree or disagree by deleting either 'True' or 'False' after each one. Remember, your first response is the important one, so do the exercise quickly.

1   Most of the difficulties experienced by deaf people would be solved if only the government would supply the money for special hearing aids.
    True/False

2   Deaf people have better eyesight to compensate for their lack of hearing.
    True/False

3   Deaf people pay a reduced television licence fee.
    True/False

4   Deaf people are well known for being faithful and loyal friends.
    True/False

5   Deaf people are allowed to have a driving licence.
    True/False

6   Deaf people are allowed to become teachers, but only of deaf children.
    True/False

7   Deaf people can understand what hearing people say by watching their lips.
    True/False

8   Deaf children do as well as hearing children in mainstream schools as long as they have good quality hearing aids.
    True/False

9   Sign language is a simple form of English produced on the hands.
    True/False

10 Gatherings of deaf people are characterized by their quietness.
    True/False

11 Medical science will soon have a cure for deafness.
    True/False

12 Deaf people are allowed a firearms licence.
    True/False

13 Deaf people's main source of information about the world is through reading.
    True/False

14 Educated deaf people communicate mostly by spelling out words on their fingers.
    True/False

15 The real tragedy of deafness is not being able to hear the birds sing or a beautiful melody.
    True/False

16 Deaf people are prevented from adopting children.
    True/False

17 Deaf people are allowed to become Members of Parliament.
   True/False

18 Deaf people are called for jury service as often as hearing people.
   True/False

19 When you meet a deaf person it is important to speak very slowly and clearly.
   True/False

20 Deaf people are particularly sensitive and empathic to others.
   True/False

Deaf people are excluded from certain occupations. Which of the following do you feel may be considered unsuitable for deaf people and why?

Δ bank manager — *telephone - meeting people*

Δ airline pilot — *radio*

Δ member of an Open University course team

Δ solicitor — *telephone - legal jargon - people*

Δ member of the armed forces — *radio - team work - oral comms*

Δ doctor — *people comms*

Δ fire officer — *radio - danger - people*

Δ train driver or signals operator — *radio -*

Δ nursery nurse — *comms*

Δ motor mechanic ◄ *hear engine - comms*

When you have finished Activity 3, the next task is to check your answers. Some of the above statements can be answered simply, others cannot and require a much more complex response. The information you need is available in a number of different places. For example, a visit to a Deaf club will help you with number 10. Reading a book[1] about deaf people and their communication will help you with numbers 7 and 9. For many of the statements it is important to go beyond the simple factual answers and this is one of the main aims of this course. Take number 5, for example. It is the case that deaf people are 'allowed' to have a driving licence. However, not all driving schools will accept deaf people or are capable of teaching them appropriately, and some insurance companies refuse to insure deaf people, while others may penalize them. And what about Heavy Goods Vehicle Licences?

It is necessary to be especially careful about the answers you thought were easy or that you already knew. Prejudices are very deeply seated and are usually about taken-for-granted things. We would recommend that you do not skip over the exercise or leave checking your answers until later in the course; the more you begin to identify and understand your attitudes and beliefs, the more interesting you will find the following units.

We recognize that among those studying this course there will be a range of experience and knowledge about deafness. Some of you will be deaf

---

[1] Either of the Set Books or the books from the Introductory Book List in the *Study Skills and Resource Booklet* should help you with this.

yourselves, some of you may have personal relationships with deaf people, while others of you may be professionals working in the area of deafness. Some of you may have no first-hand experience but a general interest in the issues raised by the course. This broad range is reflected in the course team which comprises both deaf and hearing people from a variety of backgrounds who have worked together and contributed their varied experience to the course materials.

◄ Activity 4

At this point we want you to consider the impact a course such as this might have on other students with a different experience from yours. Select two of the groups from those listed below:

Δ   A person in their twenties who has been deaf from birth.

Δ   The parents of a newly diagnosed deaf child.

Δ   Someone in their fifties who suddenly, a year ago, found themselves deaf.

Before reading further, make some notes on what you think the issues might be for them as students of the course. Then, make some notes on *your* reasons for studying this course. Why a course on deafness? Why this particular course? In what areas of the course are you particularly interested? What do you hope to achieve by the end of the course?

Keep these notes with you as you study the course. You may want to add to, or change, your reasons for studying and your interests and aims. At the end of the course you may wish to use your notes to reflect on where and why you altered your original ideas. ◄

◄ Reading

You may have found the previous tasks difficult without some help. At this point we would like you to read a number of articles on the personal experiences of some deaf people which should clarify some of the issues. All the articles are in Reader One. (You may find it helpful to review Section 3.3 on reading in the *Study Skills and Resource Booklet* at this stage.)

3.2.92

Article 6, 'The Chance to Speak for Ourselves' by Heather MacDonald;

3.2.92

Article 7, 'Deafness: The Treatment' by Lorraine Fletcher.

The articles by Heather MacDonald and Lorraine Fletcher are on opposite sides of the communication methods debate in the education of deaf children. What issues do they raise regarding parents of deaf children? What responsibilities do these parents have? And what are the pressures upon them?

1-2.93

Article 11, 'Life at Secondary School' by Elizabeth Craddock;

3-2-93

Article 13, 'Education for Life?' by Christopher Reid;

3.2.92

Article 14, 'Training to Teach' by Sarah Elsey.

Elizabeth Craddock and Christopher Reid both attended Mary Hare Grammar School. In reflecting on their school career they both regret the lack of sign language in the classroom and argue that deaf children need a more comprehensive social preparation from education, particularly regarding the Deaf community. Elizabeth Craddock's family is deaf, Christopher Reid's hearing; how do you think this may have affected the way they experienced school and their transition to adulthood? Sarah Elsey's perceptions of her deafness are very different. Why do you think this is?

Deaf v Hearing
community
where belong -
how far apart   *parent support*
latter.

3.2.93
diff

3.2.93

Article 22, 'How I Live with Deaf-Blindness' by Patrick Murphy.

To be deaf-blind is more than simply the combination of deafness and blindness, as Patrick Murphy illustrates in his account. How do you think deaf-blind people relate to the Deaf community? And what services do you think deaf-blind people require?

'more comms - less undr

Article 30, 'The Silent House' by Jack Ashley.

This article raises different issues from the others you have read. You should try to identify these issues, and consider why they are different. What would you think Jack Ashley's relationship is to the Deaf community as described by Sandra? This is discussed in more detail in Section 3. ◀

'non-exist to begin with

Hearing person who becomes deaf but would grow grad jaws Deaf Comms.

The Reader articles are not 'typical' experiences of deafness because there are no 'typical' experiences of deafness any more than there are 'typical' experiences of being hearing. They are the unique personal experiences of the authors of the articles and, as such, are valid in themselves. However, they highlight a number of important points in the lives of deaf people, a range of differences and different opinions. Now return to the exercise you have just completed in Activity 4. Would you approach the exercise differently after having read the Reader articles? What insights have you gained from reading the articles? And, are the differences simply factual or informational, or are they to do with a different way of looking at things born of a personal experience?

3 Who are Deaf people?

The focus at the beginning of this unit was on people who are born deaf, and the video *Sandra's Story* introduced you to a family who, all apart from the baby, were born deaf and who are members of the Deaf community. However, from the Reader articles you have just read you will have realized that not all people who are born deaf see deafness in the same way and not all use sign language. For example, Elizabeth Craddock, although she went to a school which used spoken language for education, clearly prefers sign language and says, 'It was pointless using a hearing aid because of my degree of hearing loss'. Yet Sarah Elsey depends upon her hearing aid and uses spoken language. She says, 'I now try to treat my hearing loss as a minor handicap'. You have also just read the article by Jack Ashley, in which he talks about returning to the House of Commons after losing his hearing, and clearly this is yet again a different situation. In addition, you may be wondering about those people who gradually go deaf with increasing age; after all, a person of 70 is more likely than not to have some hearing loss.

In common usage, then, the description 'deaf' is applied to a wide range of people. Other terms are also used: hard of hearing; people with a hearing loss; people with hearing impairment. The main distinguishing features would seem to be the degree of the hearing loss and whether a person was born deaf or became deaf later in life. These are shown in Tables 1.1 and 1.2. (You may find it helpful to consult Section 3.5 'Making sense of tables' in the *Study Skills and Resource Booklet*, at this stage, particularly as Tables 1.1 and 1.2 are used to illustrate the analysis.)

why lower?

Table 1.1 Percentage of people in the population having a hearing loss of 25 decibels or more in the better ear

Age	17–20	21–30	31–40	41–50	51–60	61–70	71+
Percentage	3	1	5	10	23	34	74

(Source: Institute of Hearing Research, in Davies, 1983)

Table 1.2 Number of people in the population with particular degrees of hearing loss

Loss in decibels	20–39	40–59	60–79	80–99	100
Number	7–8 m	2 m	66,000	132,000	44,000

(Source: Institute of Hearing Research, in DHSS, 1988)

It is not necessary for you to understand what the degree of hearing loss means in real terms except to note that the greater the loss in decibels, the more severe the hearing loss. Different degrees of hearing loss are considered in more detail in Unit 5. All you need to appreciate at this stage from examining Tables 1.1 and 1.2 is that most people with a hearing loss are elderly, with numbers rising steeply after the age of 60, and that the majority of people with a hearing loss have a minor loss. Most people's understanding of deafness or personal knowledge of deafness will focus on those who become deaf later in life. However, you will probably realize from the way in which this course started with Sandra's story, that, in the main, the group of deaf people to be considered in this and the following units is not made up of those who become deaf later in life. You may have started to think about this in Section 2, particularly when you examined the statements about deaf people in Activity 3.

At one level it is easy to define the focus of this course—namely, those people who are born deaf, who identify with the Deaf community and who use sign language, and not those who lose their hearing as they grow older, who live their lives in the hearing world and communicate through spoken language be it English, Welsh, Urdu or Greek. The easier way to reach an estimate of the size of the Deaf community is to consider all those born with a major hearing loss. About one in 1,000 people are born each year with such a loss, giving a population in the UK of about 55,000 in all. The majority of these belong to and identify with the Deaf community.

Beyond these simple distinctions between the hearing and Deaf worlds, however, definitions of the Deaf community become more complicated. What about, for example, people who in their youth or middle age lose almost all their hearing? And what about those born deaf, who do not belong to the Deaf community, do not use sign language, but do not seem to belong to the hearing world either?

While the focus of the course is on those deaf people who are members of the Deaf community, the groups mentioned above will also be considered during the year. Units 2 and 3 focus on the Deaf community and its language, for example, but Unit 4 moves beyond to look at those who have a hearing loss and do not belong to either the Deaf or hearing communities or who, for various reasons, move between the two.

Unit 5, on education, includes all children with a hearing loss who require some specialist attention within the education service. Many of these children will acquire spoken language as their means of communication and grow up to be part of the hearing world. However, in the education system they all come under the auspices of the same service.

Those people who become profoundly deaf in their early life or middle age are again different. Most will continue to live their lives in the hearing world, though their deafness may result in significant changes to their lives—Jack Ashley, in the Reader One article, for example, describes how his return to the House of Commons was a major event for him. While this group is not discussed at length in the course, an appreciation of the issues discussed is relevant to an understanding of their particular situation.[2]

The definition we seem to arrive at for the focus of the course includes all those who through their hearing loss do not identify with the hearing world and will thus be considered as deaf. Such a definition has parallels in the Black community, where the simplest definition of a Black person is someone who is not white. Beyond that there are other definitions, depending upon such matters as whether the person is from the Afro-Caribbean or Asian communities, for instance, or whether the person has Black parents, or one Black and one white parent and so on. With regard to adoption, the best placement for a child of Black and white parents is usually considered to be with a Black, rather than a white, family.

However, our problems of definition do not end here, for while it seems that we are simply talking about those born with a significant hearing loss, the Deaf community itself does not define itself by audiological criteria. Rather, the Deaf community defines itself as a cultural group, and it is therefore identification with the culture rather than with the degree of hearing loss which is the issue. The criterion for membership of the community is one of attitude rather than one of measured hearing loss. For Deaf people, the main distinguishing features of the Deaf community are the use of British Sign Language as the first or preferred language and identification with the Deaf community rather than with the hearing world. The issue of who is Deaf in this cultural sense is a central issue for this course.

The use of categories, and these questions of definitions, and the implications of definitions, are difficult issues. At this stage it is probably more important for you to understand which group the course is *not* about than what it is about. You will find that definitions of deafness are a recurring theme of the course.

◀ Reading
We would like you now to read some further articles from Reader One on the personal experiences of deaf people. Start by reading Article 1, 'Janet's Diary' by Janet Goodwill. Make some notes as you read. Look particularly for decisions that

[2] Students wishing to know more about this particular group are advised to read the excellent book by L. Jones, J. Kyle and P.L. Wood, *Words Apart*, London, Tavistock Publications, 1987. This is not required reading for the course.

were made, or events which you think have helped shape the outcome. Make some analysis of why things developed as they did, and why people talked and behaved in certain ways. (You will find it useful to adopt this approach to all Reader articles and videos on this course.)

Next read Article 24, 'Growing up in Care' by Andrew Charles and Rachel Coombs, and follow that by reading Article 9, 'School Experiences' by Clive Mason. These are two accounts of deaf children growing up. Their experiences are very different and their unfolding stories follow distinct and contrasting paths. Consider especially what developments or events you think were an inevitable consequence of deafness, or the fact that Andrew is Afro-Caribbean and Clive is white Scottish. Also, to what extent was the turn of events determined by the differing perceptions of others of deafness, ethnic origin and class?

Finally, read Article 23, 'A Deaf-Gay Man' by David Nyman, and Article 31, 'Acquired Hearing Loss: Acquired Oppression' by Maggie Woolley. Both of these accounts relate to the ideas about who Deaf people are and to some of the issues raised in Video One about Deaf clubs and the Deaf community.

There is no exercise attached to these readings; they are a varied selection of accounts of deaf people and their experiences. Their significance at this stage is that they identify some important areas for enquiry, and they illustrate a diversity amongst the Deaf community that should help to counteract some of the negative stereotypical images of deaf people that exist in our society. ◄

3.1 Is it 'Deaf' or 'deaf'?

You may have noticed in the unit so far that sometimes deaf is spelt with an upper case 'D' (Deaf) and at other times with a lower case 'd' (deaf) and that this does not follow the usual conventions of written English. The convention this use of upper and lower case aims to observe is one that is being increasingly adopted by Deaf people; namely, an upper case 'D' is used to indicate those Deaf people who identify themselves as part of a cultural and linguistic group, the Deaf community. It is similar to the way that an upper case 'J' would be appropriate when referring to a Jewish person, or an upper case 'B' for a Brazilian, for example. For a similar reason you will notice we also usually use the upper case 'B' when talking about the Black community.

As Padden and Humphries write:

> Before beginning our journey through the imagery and patterns of meaning that constitute Deaf people's lives, we must identify the community of 'Deaf' people with which we are concerned. Following a convention proposed by James Woodward (1972), we use the lowercase *deaf* when referring to the audiological condition of not hearing, and the uppercase *Deaf* when referring to a particular group of deaf people who share a language—American Sign Language (ASL)—and a culture. The members of this group reside in the United States and Canada, have inherited their sign language, use it as a primary means of communication among themselves, and hold a set of beliefs about themselves and their connection to the larger society. We distinguish them from, for example, those who find themselves losing their hearing because of illness, trauma or age; although these people share the condition of not hearing, they do not have access to the knowledge, beliefs, and practices that make up the culture of Deaf

people. ... this knowledge of Deaf people is not simply a camaraderie with others who have a similar physical condition, but is, like many other cultures in the traditional sense of the term, historically created and actively transmitted across generations.

Woodward's distinction, while useful, is not an entirely clear-cut one. For example, consider deaf children from hearing families who encounter Deaf people and their culture outside the family. At what point are they said to have adopted the conventions of the culture and become Deaf? This question also applies to the acculturation processes of deaf adults who, after spending many years apart from Deaf people, come to join the community at later ages. Markowicz and Woodward (1978) have suggested that self-identification with the group and skill in ASL should be important diagnostic factors in deciding who is Deaf. But the bounded distinction between the terms *Deaf* and *deaf* represents only part of the dynamic of how Deaf people talk about themselves. Deaf people are both Deaf and deaf, and their discussions, even arguments, over issues of identity show that these two categories are often interrelated in complex ways. ... these complexities ... [include] the cases of two groups who pose special problems for the culture: newly arrived deaf persons who have yet to learn the full range of skills required for the culture, and hearing children from Deaf families. A newly arrived deaf person is often given one of several borderline labels, such as 'hard of hearing', recognizing his or her past affiliation with those who speak. Hearing children of Deaf parents represent an ongoing contradiction in the culture: they display the knowledge of their parents—skill in the language and social conduct—but the culture finds subtle ways to give them an unusual and separate status.

Also following Woodward, we use the term *Deaf* ... to refer to other cultures of people who do not hear and who use sign languages other than ASL. In Quebec, for example, Deaf French Canadians use a different sign language, Langue des Signes Québecois. Nova Scotia has a community of Deaf people whose sign language is related to British Sign Language but not to ASL. In fact, in nearly every nation in the world there are several distinct groups of Deaf people, their differences marked by political, historical, or geographical separation.

(Padden and Humphries, 1988)

This paper by Padden and Humphries formed the basis for a course team agenda item during the writing of this course and it was agreed that the rationale for the distinction between the use of the two terms described should be adopted as course policy and that course material authors would use it. It is an attempt to refer to Deaf people in the way that they themselves would wish. However, as a policy its application is not straightforward, so where its use is not clear the view of Deaf consultants to the course has been accepted. The difficulties in applying this convention will be discussed later in the course. These relate particularly to its use with children.

3.2 Transcription of British Sign Language

A different, but related issue is how British Sign Language, or BSL, is represented in a written form. As there is no written form of BSL and, anyway, this course is in written English, an agreement needed to be reached on how the contributions of deaf people would be presented in the course texts. Anyone who has bought a radio, television, or some other piece of technology manufactured in the Far East, will be familiar with some of the errors that can occur in a translation from Japanese or Chinese to English. And, whilst this may be mildly amusing (or simply confusing), the amusement is usually at the expense of the person who did the translation and whose first language is not English.

The problem here is not that this person is unintelligent (although this may be the assumption); rather, it is that the 'signs' of language (the words) are arbitrary and culturally bound and often it is impossible to translate directly, word for word, from one language to another. For example, how would you translate the phrase 'a stiff upper lip' to a non-English speaking Peruvian without a fairly comprehensive explanation of English culture?

In order to overcome similar difficulties with regard to BSL in the writing of this course, it was decided that, when the *content* of the translation was the significant element, in the author's view, it should be presented in standard English; only on the few occasions when a point about the structure of language was being made would the transcription remain literal. You have already encountered an example of this in 'Growing up in Care', Article 24 by Andrew Charles and Rachel Coombs in Reader One. The original account was given in BSL to a video camera and was then translated into standard English.

4 Changing attitudes to deafness

◄ Activity 5
Note down as many sayings as you can that include the word 'deaf'. ◄

You may have thought of such sayings as 'deaf as a post' or 'deaf as a door-nail'. Most will have negative connotations. The words used to describe deaf people—for example, 'deaf and dumb', 'stone deaf' and 'deaf-mute'—also create a particular image.

These images are also negative; the word 'dumb', for example, is often used to mean 'stupid' and the image that therefore comes across is that deaf people lack intelligence. The major organizations for deaf people have dropped the term 'dumb' from their title as a consequence—the British Deaf Association, for instance, changed its name from the British Deaf and Dumb Association in 1971.

The press often still uses the term 'deaf and dumb', thus reinforcing the negative images, although these days it is likely to get a reaction from one of the major deaf organizations, as the following letter shows:

Profoundly deaf people are not dumb, says RNID[3]

Sir—I hope I will not be alone among your readership to protest at your use of the phrase 'deaf and dumb' in the New Focus article on violence (Community Care 11 August).

We at the Royal National Institute for the Deaf live in constant hope that this inaccurate and offensive phrase has finally been eradicated from journalists' vocabulary and, indeed, there has been progress. Even the tabloids tend to avoid using it these days, so it is particularly distressing to find it printed bold in your pages.

Deaf people are not dumb in the medical sense, if they do not speak it is because they are pre-lingually, profoundly deaf and have never heard, nor learnt to understand the spoken word.

Nor are they 'dumb' in the colloquial American sense of the word; that is, stupid, of limited intelligence. But it is inevitable that this kind of connection be made when people who have no experience or understanding of deafness read this iniquitous phrase.

The best way to refer to a deaf person without speech is to call them 'profoundly deaf', which indeed you do in your Personnel file section only a few pages further on.

(Stuart Etherington, Director, Advocacy and Information, Royal National Institute for the Deaf)

Editor's note: Apologies! We used the term believing deaf mute to be archaic and thinking that lay people (who would, for these purposes, include non-specialist readers) would think profoundly deaf a synonym for very deaf. However, we accept the RNID's view and will on future occasions adopt 'profoundly deaf'.

(*Community Care*, 1 September 1988)

In the past, deaf people were often thought of as incapable. Little is known of the status of deaf people in early history, except in Europe, where what is documented suggests that deaf people were deprived of many rights—to inherit property, for instance; or to take part in Mass; or marry without the permission of the Pope. This seems to have been the position in the Middle Ages and until the sixteenth century. It is interesting, though, that the Justinian code of AD 530, which is often cited as a main vehicle for the deprivation of rights, in fact recognized that deafness and lack of competence were not linked. It gave full rights to:

1   Deaf people who, though without speech, were literate.
2   Deaf people who could speak.
3   Those without speech who could hear.
4   Those who became deaf.

[3] Royal National Institute for the Deaf.

However, after the fall of Rome deaf people were again excluded from many rights, until the development of education for deaf children in the sixteenth century. The early thrust for this education was to teach deaf people to speak, to enable them to retain their rights. The honour of being the first teacher of the deaf is generally given to Pablo Ponce de Leon, who tutored the children of the Spanish aristocracy, amongst whom deafness was relatively common. His first pupil was Don Francisco Velasco, eldest son of the heir to the House of Tudor, who would not be allowed to inherit because he could not speak and thus was unable to confess his sins and gain absolution. Through de Leon's tuition Valasco learnt to speak and gained his lawful inheritance. The denial to deaf people of particular rights under law is not new and still occurs in some places. For example, in Spain deaf people are classified as mentally ill and cannot buy houses or flats in their own name (Jones and Pullen, 1987). Also, the European Parliament has recently tried to pass laws preventing deaf people from driving heavy goods vehicles, although this has met with considerable opposition from organizations of deaf people in this country, particularly the British Deaf Association, and throughout Europe.

ITQ

Consider the articles you have read and the video *Sandra's Story*. What factors contribute to deafness being perceived either as a problem or not as a problem? *Misunderstanding, lack of hearing knowledge of deaf + BSL, difference, comms*

One of the factors you may have identified that created deafness as a problem was the demand, or expectations, of the hearing world. But this is not inevitable, as the following extract describing the life of deaf people on Martha's Vineyard shows:

> One of Gale Huntington's favourite activities is driving his guests around the island of Martha's Vineyard, Massachusetts, at speed never exceeding thirty-five miles an hour, and pointing out spots of historical interest. Gale's memory of the region goes back over eighty years, when coasting vessels crowded Vineyard Haven harbor and whale ships were still seen in New Bedford. He knows as much about the Island as anyone alive today. In the course of one of these jaunts 'up-Island', in late October 1978, Gale pointed out Jedidiah's house to me. 'He was a good neighbor,' said Gale, 'He used to fish and farm some. He was one of the best dory men on the Island, and that was pretty good, considering he had only one hand.'
>
> What happened to the other one?' I asked.
>
> 'Lost it in a mowing machine accident when he was a teenager.'
>
> As an afterthought, he added, 'he was deaf and dumb too.'
>
> 'Because of the accident?' I asked.
>
> 'Oh no,' said Gale, 'he was born that way.'
>
> On the way back to Vineyard Haven, as we puttered down a sandy ridge overlooking a wide expanse of Vineyard Sound, Gale glanced at a weatherbeaten clapboard house on the left and said 'Jedidiah's brother lived there.' Nathaniel had owned a large dairy farm. 'And,'

said Gale, putting his foot on the brakes by way of emphasis, 'he was considered a very wealthy man—at least by Chilmark standards. Come to think of it, he was deaf and dumb too.'

I wondered aloud why both brothers had been born deaf. Gale said no one had ever known why; perhaps the deafness was inherited. I suggested that it might have been caused by disease. But Gale didn't think so, because there were so many deaf people up-Island, and they were all related. There had been deaf Vineyarders as long as anyone could remember. The last one died in the early 1950s.

How many deaf people were there?' I asked.

'Oh,' said Gale, 'I can remember six right offhand, no, seven.'

'How many people lived in town here then?'

' Maybe two hundred,' Gale replied, 'maybe two hundred fifty. Not more than that.'

I remarked that that seemed to be a very large number of deaf people in such a small community. Gale seemed surprised but added that he too had occasionally been struck by the fact that there were so many deaf people. No one else in town had treated this as unusual, however, so he had thought little more about it.

One rainy afternoon on my next trip to Martha's Vineyard, I sat down with Gale and tried to figure out the genealogies of the deaf Islanders whom he remembered. I thought that the deafness up-Island might have been the result of an inherited trait for deafness, and I wanted to do some research on the topic.

Gale's knowledge of Island history and genealogy was extensive. He sat in his living room smoking a few of those cigarettes expressly forbidden by his doctor and taking more than a few sips of his favorite New England rum as he reminisced about items long passed and friends who had been dead half a century or more. As we talked, he recalled from his childhood three or four additional deaf people. When he was a boy in the early 1900s, ten deaf people lived in the town of Chilmark alone.

I had already spent a good part of the afternoon copying down various genealogies before I thought to ask Gale what the hearing people in town had thought of the deaf people.

'Oh,' he said, 'they didn't think anything about them, they were just like everyone else.'

'But how did people communicate with them—by writing everything down?'

'No,' said Gale, surprised that I should ask such an obvious question. 'You see, everyone here spoke sign language.'

'You mean the deaf people's families and such?' I inquired.

'Sure,' Gale replied, as he wandered into the kitchen to refill his glass and find some more matches, 'and everybody else in town too—I used to speak it, my mother did, everybody.'

...

A deaf person's greatest problem is not simply that he or she cannot hear but that the lack of hearing is socially isolating. The deaf person's knowledge and awareness of the larger society are limited because hearing people find it difficult or impossible to communicate with him or her. Even if the deaf person knows sign language, only a very small percentage of the hearing population can speak it and can communicate easily with deaf people. The difficulty in communicating, along with the ignorance and misinformation about deafness that is pervasive in most of the hearing world, combine to cause difficulties in all aspects of life for deaf individuals—in education, employment, community involvement, and civil rights.

On the Vineyard, however, the hearing people were bilingual in English and the Island sign language. This adaptation had more than linguistic significance, for it eliminated the wall that separates the most deaf people from the rest of society. How well can deaf people integrate themselves into the community if no communication barriers exist and if everyone is familiar and comfortable with deafness? The evidence from the Island indicates that they are extremely successful at this.

One of the strongest indications that the deaf were completely integrated into all aspects of society is that in all the interviews I conducted, deaf Islanders were never thought of or referred to as a group or as 'the deaf'. Every one of the deaf people who is remembered today is thought of as a unique individual. When I inquired about 'the deaf' or asked informants to list all the deaf people they had known, most could remember only one or two, although many of them had known more than that. I was able to elicit comments about specific individuals only by reading informants a list of all the deaf people known to have lived on the Island. My notes show a good example of this when, in an interview with a woman who is now in her early nineties, I asked, 'Do you know anything similar about Isaiah and David?'

'Oh yes!' she replied. 'They both were very good fishermen, very good indeed.'

'Weren't they both deaf?' I prodded.

'Yes, come to think of it, I guess they both were,' she replied. 'I'd forgotten about that.'

On the mainland profound deafness is regarded as a true handicap, but I suggest that a handicap is defined by the community in which it appears. Although we can categorize the deaf Vineyarders as disabled, they certainly were not considered to be handicapped. They participated freely in all aspects of life in this Yankee community. They grew up, married, raised their families, and earned their livings in just the same manner as did their hearing relatives, friends, and neighbors. As one older man on the Island remarked, 'I didn't think about the deaf any more than you'd think about anybody with a different voice.'

> Perhaps the best description of the status of deaf individuals on the Vineyard was given to me by an island woman in her eighties, when I asked about those who were handicapped by deafness when she was a girl. 'Oh,' she said emphatically, 'those people weren't handicapped. They were just deaf.'

(Groce, 1985)

To be deaf was not a problem, not even an issue for the inhabitants of Martha's Vineyard at that time. Yet in our current society deafness *is* perceived as a problem, at least by hearing people.

Vic Finkelstein has described how a society can be organized in such a way as to create a problem, by writing an article about a community in which everyone was in a wheelchair. Doors were built at a height of five foot and ceilings at seven foot four inches. The society was then joined by a few able-bodied people. He describes the consequences for those who were able-bodied thus:

> Naturally, one of the first things they noticed was the heights of the doors and ceilings. They noticed this directly, by constantly knocking their heads on the door lintels. Soon all the able-bodied members of the village were also marked by the dark bruises they carried on their foreheads. Of course, they went to see the village doctors, who were, naturally, also wheelchair-users. Soon the wheelchair-user doctors, wheelchair-user psychiatrist, wheelchair-user social workers, etc., were involved in the problems of the able-bodied villagers. The doctors produced learned reports about the aches and pains of the able-bodied in society. They saw how the bruises and painful backs (from walking bent double so frequently) were *caused* by their physical condition. The wheelchair-user doctors analysed the problems and wrote their definitions. They said these able-bodied people suffered a 'loss or reduction of functional ability' which resulted in a handicap. This handicap caused a 'disadvantage or restriction of activity' which made them disabled in this society.

> Soon special aids were designed by the wheelchair-user doctors and associated professions for the able-bodied disabled members of the village. All the able-bodied were given special toughened helmets (provided free by the village) to wear at all times. Special braces were designed which gave support while keeping the able-bodied wearer bent at a height similar to their fellow wheelchair-user villagers. Some doctors went so far as to suggest that there was no hope for these poor sufferers unless they too used wheelchairs, and one person even went so far as to suggest amputation to bring the able-bodied down to the right height! The able-bodied disabled caused many problems. When they sought jobs no one would employ them. Special experts had to be trained to understand these problems and new professions created for their care. When one able-bodied disabled person applied for a job as a television interviewer, a special medical examination had to be arranged to see whether he was fit for this work. In the end it was decided that he was not suitable. It was felt, the wheelchair-user doctor pointed out in the case file, that a television interviewer wearing a helmet all the time would not be acceptable. Since the cameras would only show the top of his head (because the able-bodied were always bent double by the harnesses they had to wear) he would

not be suitable for interviewing. It is well known, the wheelchair-user doctor wrote, how difficult it is to communicate with the able-bodied because it is not easy to see their facial expressions and meet eye-to-eye while they are bent double.

In time special provision had to be made in the village to provide a means of obtaining money for these able-bodied disabled to live. Voluntary societies were created to collect charity and many shops and pubs had an upturned helmet placed on the counters for customers to leave their small change. Painted on the helmets were the words 'Help the able-bodied disabled'. Sometimes a little plaster-cast model would stand in the corner of the shop—the figure bent double, in their characteristic pose, with a slotted box on the figure's back for small coins.

(Finkelstein, 1981)

Such a reversal of the usual roles makes it clear how a disability can be created. In the conclusion to Finkelstein's article the 'able-bodied disabled' organize themselves to fight for changes in attitude and for social change. However, even this was seen by some as the able-bodied disabled failing to accept their disability.

There are clear parallels here with the way deafness is understood by the hearing majority in our society.

 ◀ Activity 6
You should attempt to describe a world in which everybody is deaf—no one can hear anything at all.

How is it different?

What would happen to hearing people who had to join? ◀

5 Popular conceptions of deafness

5.1 The silent world of the deaf

Almost at the root
Of that tall pine, the shadow of whose bare
And slender stem, while here I sit at eve,
Oft stretches toward me, like a long straight path
Traced faintly in the greensward; there, beneath
A plain blue stone, a gentle Dalesman lies,
From whom, in early childhood, was withdrawn
The precious gift of hearing. He grew up
From year to year in loneliness of soul;
And this deep mountain-valley was to him
Soundless, with all its streams. The bird of dawn
Did never rouse this Cottager from sleep
With startling summons; not for his delight
The vernal cuckoo shouted; not for him
Murmured the labouring bee. When stormy winds
Were working the broad bosom of the lake
Into a thousand, thousand sparkling waves,
Rocking the trees, or driving cloud on cloud
Along the sharp edge of yon lofty crags,
The agitated scene before his eye
Was silent as a picture: evermore
Were all things silent, wheresoe'er he moved.

(William Wordsworth, 1770–1850, From *The Excursion,* Book VII)

"*Could I but Hear*"
3901
by J. Kemp. Deaf. artist

Figure 1.10

(Source: courtesy of the Royal National Institute for the Deaf)

In this poem, Wordsworth exemplifies one of the most popular notions of deafness, that Deaf people live in a silent world, and that the 'tragedy' of deafness is not being able to hear the sounds of nature.

This is clearly a hearing perspective—that is, when hearing people think of deafness this is what it means to them. But the world of the deaf is not silent, and, more importantly, sound or lack of sound is not an issue for them; rather, it is something imposed from the hearing view of deafness.

ITQ
Consider Sandra, her family and friends. How appropriate is it to think of them in terms of what they cannot hear?

In the light of what you have just read, it would be wholly inappropriate to think of Sandra and her family and friends in terms of what they cannot hear. Yet the notion of silence and sound pervades much of the thinking about deafness: not just the popular notions, but the professional views as well. The titles of journals about deafness indicate this clearly as in, for example, *Hark, Talk, Hearing, The Silent Messenger* and *Soundbarrier;* while some of these are now defunct, some are still in existence. In a former RNID advertising campaign the word 'hear' was a feature of the copy, as Figure 1.11 illustrates. The emphasis here is on what is missing in hearing terms, rather than on positive constructions of deafness.

Figure 1.11 'Let's hear it for the RNID'
(Source: courtesy of the Royal National Institute for the Deaf)

5.2 Public images of deafness

◀ Activity 7
Ask a number of people (about twenty), hearing and deaf (if possible), men and women, and covering a range of ages, the following:

(a) How many deaf people do you know?

(b) Can you name five deaf public figures?

(c) What do you think it is like to be deaf? ◀

The responses to your questions in this activity will obviously differ according to whom you ask, and their knowledge and understanding of deafness. Deaf people may describe deafness in terms of membership of the Deaf community, use of sign language and so forth. They may name similar public figures to those named by hearing people or they may also name leaders in the Deaf community.

Hearing people who are unfamiliar with Deaf people may well confirm the stereotypes already discussed. They may not differentiate between those born deaf and those who become deaf. They may focus their replies concerning what it is like to be deaf on non-hearing. More interesting will be the deaf people that they name. In the experience of the course team the three most likely to occur are Beethoven, Helen Keller and Jack Ashley, all of whom would not be seen as members of the Deaf community. Most hearing people will have difficulty in naming more, though others could be Evelyn Glennie or Elizabeth Quinn.

◀ Activity 8
Pause for a moment at this point and reflect on the concept of a deaf person that would emerge from the responses to your questions in Activity 7. ◀

There has been one government survey of 'Public Attitudes to Deafness' which was conducted on behalf of the then Department of Health and Social Security by Claire Bunting in 1981 (Bunting, 1981). Unfortunately for us, and possibly for the Department, Bunting did not distinguish between attitudes to Deaf people and attitudes to those who are hard of hearing, although she does report that the experience of deafness of most of the individuals mentioned was with the 'partially deaf' (45%) rather than the 'totally deaf' (8%). The other respondents reported contact with both groups.

The report shows that people in general have very little understanding of deafness. What is more significant, however, is the way in which the questions themselves, as they were constructed, led people in to thinking about deafness as problematic. The following three examples illustrate this point:

> Would you rate total deafness as a very severe, severe, moderate or mild handicap?
>
> Do you think deaf people try to hide the fact that they are deaf?
>
> Would you say a deaf person's voice or speech differs from that of someone who can hear properly?
>
> (Bunting, 1981)

[handwritten margin notes: "hearing world q's" / "What do you consider are the main handicaps / problems for a deaf person in a hearing world?"]

ITQ
You should reflect upon these questions in the context of the video about Sandra's family and the articles by Elizabeth Craddock and Christopher Reid that you have already read in Reader One. How does that view of deafness contrast with the view embodied in the survey questions above? What bias is introduced into a survey using such questions? What could more appropriate questions be?

Sandra Smith, Elizabeth Craddock and Christopher Reid see themselves as part of a cultural group, the 'Deaf community', in which their deafness is not a problem but a part of their lives. The Bunting survey takes for granted that deafness is a problem, a disability, and the investigation is of the extent of the problem. The Bunting survey can therefore only find deafness to be a problem. If you find it difficult to think of more appropriate questions, you may find it helpful to review Video One and see how deafness is discussed there.

5.3 Popular stereotypes of deafness

One of the most readily available sources of information about deafness is the press.

◀ Activity 9
You should read carefully the newspaper items (Excerpts 1–13) in the Appendix and consider the following questions as you do so:

(a) How are deaf people portrayed in the press?

(b) What picture is given of the lives of deaf people?

(c) What problems are deaf people described as having?

(d) What is conveyed about the relationship between deaf and hearing people?

You should also reflect upon all of the excerpts in the light of your reading of Reader One and viewing of Video One. ◀

◀ Comment
First, it needs to be appreciated that the press does not distinguish between prelingually profoundly deaf people and others with a hearing loss. Most of the cuttings chosen are included because they are about those born deaf. The most remarkable fact to emerge in a reading of these excerpts is that it would never occur to one to think that deaf people are part of a Deaf community with its own language and culture. It is presented as remarkable that deaf people marry (see Excerpts 1 and 2)—'Joy as deaf couple wed', 'A love beyond words'—and that, if they have children, not hearing the baby cry or say his or her first words is presented as the major issue (see Excerpt 3).

Even the idea that deaf people can live normal lives is presented as worthy of comment—Excerpt 4, for example, states: 'They appear to live normal lives, yet Chris is profoundly deaf and his wife partially deaf'.

Many of the cuttings endorse the deaf world as being one of sadness because of what is not heard, as the following quotations show: 'Sarah and Stuart have both been locked in a world of silence since birth' (Excerpt 2); ' ... never heard each other say: "I love you"' (Excerpt 3); 'The loving couple will never hear their baby's cries nor her first words' (Excerpt 3); 'One poignant thought remained. Deaf children would never be able to hear Christmas bells or sing carols' (Excerpt 6); ' ... cannot hear the start of each race' (Excerpt 7).

The characterization of deaf people is thin, a narrow range of stereotypes. Deaf people are either brave superheroes: 'Deaf BMX Whizzkid' (Excerpt 7); 'Town rallies to aid brave Louis' (Excerpt 8); or they are victims or figures of pathos: 'A Samaritan life line for deaf victims' (Excerpt 9); 'tragically vulnerable' (Excerpt 10). A quite normal achievement can be portrayed as something special, educating the ideas that deaf people should not be expected to do various things such as driving (Excerpt 11). Even when the article itself makes the point that a special vulnerability of deaf people is not an issue, often the headline will nevertheless exploit such a possibility. In the article 'Deaf children face the risk of sexual abuse' it becomes clear that no one is claiming a special danger for deaf children; rather, the issue is to do with vetting drivers to take children to school, yet the headline carries a different message (Excerpt 12).

Most of the press coverage in 1989–90 relating to deafness focused on the operation involving cochlear implants. Nobody could guess from the publicity that the operation is only relevant for a small minority of people with a hearing loss, and while it gives some sensation of sound it does not fully restore hearing. There are numerous articles on this. The headlines include:

'Deaf to get electronic ears on NHS', *The Guardian*, 5 January 1990

'Children to lead queue for NHS bank ears', *The Sunday Times*, 7 January 1990

'Operation ends six silent years', *Hull Daily Mail*, 25 January 1990

'Bionic miracle that can bring back lost world of sound', *The Scotsman*, 12 January 1990

'Doctors to give deaf girl gift of hearing', *Sheffield Journal*, 1 February 1990

The whole issue of cochlear implants is discussed in more detail in Units 9 and 10. However, it is significant here because such a major emphasis in the press on cure reinforces the idea of deafness as disease or deformity, and as the province of doctors and technicians. Medical ideas of deafness are also reiterated by articles such as that by Rosie Barnes, 'Why I would have an abortion' (Excerpt 13), in which she says, 'My son Daniel, who has only partial hearing, was subject to tormenting jibes because of his hearing aid as soon as he started school. … He hasn't had a happy childhood, and his handicap is only mild.'

You should reflect upon your own reaction to this excerpt—in telling her story, is Rosie Barnes inadvertently reinforcing narrow ideas as to what is 'normal' and 'acceptable' and what is not? ◄

A further popular portrayal of deaf people occurs in jokes. In one told by Jasper Carrott on his BBC Television show, he started to tell a joke supposedly about deaf people. The point of the joke was that he covered his face so he could not be lipread and many judged this to be in bad taste. On the BBC TV programme 'Not the Nine O'Clock News' a deaf man was shown with new equipment which alerted him when the telephone was ringing. The equipment was elaborate, a transmitter and a large cumbersome receiver strapped to the man's head that emitted a flashing light when the 'phone rang. The main part of the joke was that when the man responded to the flashing light and picked up the 'phone and said 'Hallo', he could not understand the reply. This did not seem as tasteless. Why?

One reason could be that the first joke actually ridiculed deaf people whereas the second was targeted at an elaborate but inappropriate technological development, though with the development of visual display telephones for deaf people the concept may not have been quite so inappropriate after all.

There are, of course, many other portrayals of deaf people, in film, fiction, drama and on television, which influence the way in which deafness is understood.

◀ Activity 10
You should consider here any deaf fictional character of which you are aware and
the perception of deafness that he or she embodies.

As you go through the year you should collect as many examples as possible as these
will be discussed in more detail in Unit 8. ◀

5.4 Deaf people as 'product'—the world of advertising

The title of this section may shock, but it comes from a report by the Kings
Fund Centre, *They Aren't in the Brief* (Scott-Parker, 1989) which looks at the
ways in which charities advertise.

In the past, much of the advertising of major charities was patronising, as
Figures 1.12 and 1.13 illustrate.

Although advertisements are more sophisticated in the way in which they
portray deaf people, their content remains a focus of controversy, as the
examples of the 1988–89 advertising campaigns of both the RNID and the
Royal Association in Aid of Deaf People (RAD), shown in Figures 1.14 to
1.18, illustrate. The advertising campaigns of both the RNID and the RAD
were a feature of a 'See Hear' programme (the BBC magazine programme for
deaf people) in July 1989. In this discussion, two deaf people, Geraldine
O'Halloran and Roger Fox, challenged Mike Whitlam, Chief Executive of the
RNID and Rosemary Brotherton, Chief Executive of the RAD. The following
is an extract from their discussion:

Roger: Well, all three are bad images I think [the RAD
advertisements]. The RAD is trying to tell people what Deaf
people's problems are, they need interpreters and so on, that's
fine, but the pictures—there's one with someone's head
bandaged, it makes hearing people think that Deaf people are
deaf and dumb, they can't hear and they can't speak.

Rosemary: We were trying to get some very striking images across to the
general public, to hearing people who know very little about
deafness, the needs of profoundly Deaf people who have a
different first language. In those posters our advertising
consultant tried to reflect the concepts and feelings that Deaf
people had conveyed to him—the sense of isolation, of being
cut off, of being separated from what we describe in some of
the publicity as an uncaring society.

Geraldine: I feel strongly about the posters. I feel they show Deaf people
in a very bad way. It's a very poor image for Deaf people.
There's no Deaf pride, no Deaf culture, there's nothing about
the Deaf language, BSL, and when hearing people look at the
posters they think, what a shame, poor Deaf people, we'll pay
out some money for them. You make hearing people feel
guilty about them and you're not showing how hearing
people can become part of the Deaf community—learn to
sign.

Mike: I think the main awareness campaign—the posters that show
two ears and perhaps the brain, they are the current themes
of our main campaign, are intended to do exactly what it is

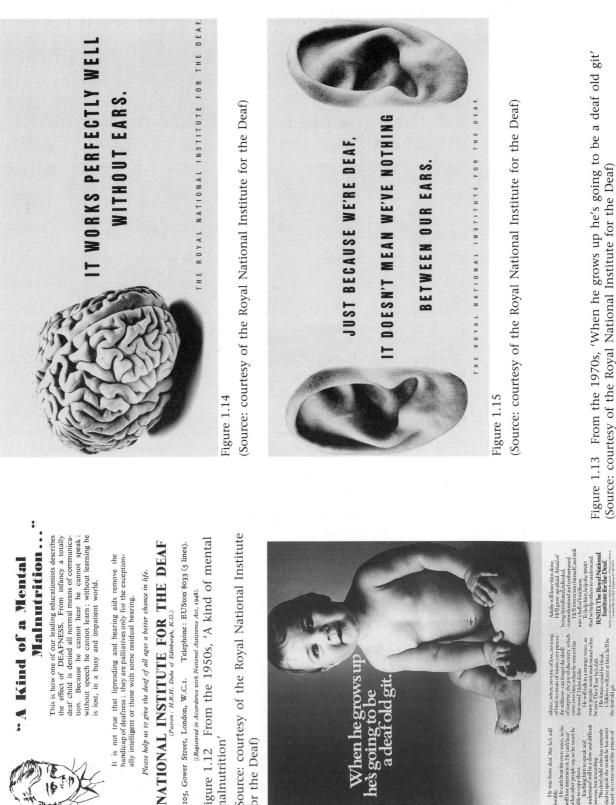

It Works Perfectly Well

IT WORKS PERFECTLY WELL
WITHOUT EARS.

THE ROYAL NATIONAL INSTITUTE FOR THE DEAF.

Figure 1.14
(Source: courtesy of the Royal National Institute for the Deaf)

JUST BECAUSE WE'RE DEAF,
IT DOESN'T MEAN WE'VE NOTHING
BETWEEN OUR EARS.

THE ROYAL NATIONAL INSTITUTE FOR THE DEAF.

Figure 1.15
(Source: courtesy of the Royal National Institute for the Deaf)

"A Kind of a Mental Malnutrition…"

This is how one of our leading educationists describes the effect of DEAFNESS. From infancy a totally deaf child is denied all normal means of communication. Because he cannot hear he cannot speak: without speech he cannot learn: without learning he is lost, in a busy and impatient world.

It is not true that lipreading and hearing aids remove the handicap of deafness: they are palliatives only for the exceptionally intelligent or those with some residual hearing.

Please help us to give the deaf of all ages a better chance in life.

NATIONAL INSTITUTE FOR THE DEAF
(Patron : H.R.H. Duke of Edinburgh, K.G.)

105, Gower Street, London, W.C.1.   Telephone: EUSton 8033 (5 lines).

[(*Registered in Accordance with National Assistance Act, 1948*).]

Figure 1.12 From the 1950s, 'A kind of mental malnutrition'

(Source: courtesy of the Royal National Institute for the Deaf)

Figure 1.13 From the 1970s, 'When he grows up he's going to be a deaf old git'
(Source: courtesy of the Royal National Institute for the Deaf)

Figure 1.17

(Source: courtesy of the Royal Association in Aid of Deaf People)

Figure 1.16

(Source: courtesy of the Royal Association in Aid of Deaf People)

we're being accused of not doing, that is actually project a very positive image of Deaf people. Now there are lots of messages that need to be projected to the public at large about the Deaf community, about sign language, about all sorts of other things, but advertising, it's something where you have to have very simple and very clear messages, very powerful messages. And we too as our first theme on the awareness campaign, the issue which seemed to be around most and that is the Deaf people were projected as stupid because they can't hear, they don't use their voice and so on, and the two posters that we've tried, the 'ears' poster and the 'brain' poster, have in fact said very much that Deaf people

Figure 1.18
(Source: courtesy of the Royal Association in Aid of Deaf People)

are not stupid, that they are as intelligent as everybody else and they should have the right of access to every service, employment and so forth. So in fact our campaign is based on the information we get and is intended to project a very positive image.

Geraldine: If the Deaf community got together they could make decisions as to how they wanted Deaf people portrayed to the world. Not leave it to hearing people how Deaf people should be portrayed. Deaf people should have more control over this. And Deaf people have to look at the posters too and decide how we feel about them, that young Deaf people, that the youngsters growing up will think, 'What an awful world. Is my life going to be like that?' It's a real sort of shock thing. It's a depressing view. There must be a way to be more positive and show the Deaf community, Deaf culture, BSL, whatever.

(Transcription from programme 8 of BBC Television 'See Hear', July 1989)

These concerns are not specific to deaf people. The Kings Fund Centre report looks at the portrayal in advertising of people with disabilities, and while some Deaf people might reject the label of disability for themselves, some of the conclusions of the report are relevant. They suggest that 'People with disabilities have no generally acknowledged right to determine the manner in which they are portrayed to the general public nor is there any routine way in which they are involved in planning or evaluating campaigns currently produced' (Scott-Parker, 1989). They point out that, because people with disabilities are not the client, not the agency and not the public, they are 'not in the brief'.

6 Conclusion

6.1 Reflections on this unit

We have introduced the course by looking at positive images of Deaf people and their community. In this way an examination of the problems that arise can be undertaken with an understanding of the Deaf community, its language and culture.

It was decided to use Video One to start the whole course because it is a way of immediately involving you in some of the issues. You have met the Smith family and were introduced to the Deaf community through their accounts of their experiences. Video One demonstrates that there is a very strong sense of history amongst the Deaf community, a history of which hearing people are often unaware, and sometimes refuse to acknowledge.

The video also raises issues about communication. Deaf people in the video were clearly expressing themselves in sign language in a very articulate manner on a range of subjects. So already you have been presented with the idea that there is a Deaf community with its own culture and language, and it is a belief in this idea that underpins the whole course. And yet, there are popular stereotypes of deaf people that do not fit with this view.

How much consideration is given to Deaf culture and language in the education of deaf children? Is, for instance, the language of the Deaf community, British Sign Language, a proper language? Or is it simply a manual form of English? Can ideas and information be transmitted effectively in an educational setting using sign language? There is clearly a view amongst many educationalists that the education of deaf children must be based in written and spoken English. This is in keeping with the integration and normalization approaches of current educational policy for all children described as having special educational needs. This will be discussed further in Unit 5. Yet, you have seen from Video One that British Sign Language is a rich and expressive language and the language of the British Deaf community. What would be the implication of using this as a means of education?

In this course you will be presented with accounts of the experiences of deaf people with health and welfare agencies. But who are the appropriate agencies for responding to the needs of deaf people? If deaf people are a linguistic community, why are they mostly categorized as a disabled group by service providers? There is a growing awareness that many more female doctors are needed to provide an appropriate response to the needs of women patients, and that many more Black teachers and social workers are needed for the Black community. The world of deaf people, however, is dominated by professionals who are hearing, and is there any indication that this situation will ever be different?

Now return to Section 2, to the self-rating exercise in Activity 2 and the statements about deaf people in Activity 3. You may already want to reconsider where you have located yourself on your scale, or some of the answers you gave to the statements, or it may be too early yet. Don't worry too much if you feel you have not progressed—this is not significant at this stage of the course. As a way of developing your understanding of the Deaf community, let us now explore in more depth three of the 'statements about deaf people' given in Activity 3.

'Deaf people can understand what hearing people say by watching their lips' (Statement 7)

Lip-reading is often cited as the 'natural' way for deaf people to communicate. As if by magic, or perhaps by biological pre-programming, they have, or can quickly acquire, the ability to understand everything that is said to them by watching the lips of the speaker.

You have already read Jack Ashley's article from Reader One. He raised problems of varying light, facial hair, group situations and performing simple functions such as eating a meal, as major obstacles to lip-reading. He also wrote about the need for 100 per cent concentration, and about eye-strain, physical exhaustion and his flagging self-confidence.

Prior to being traumatically deafened, Jack Ashley was accustomed to using spoken English to a sophisticated level—he already had the concept of communicating by speech, and knowledge of the structure of spoken English. Consider how much more difficult it must be for someone who is born deaf and has never heard spoken language.

In practice, lip-reading is an extremely difficult skill to develop. Many of the sounds of speech are produced inside the mouth and do not appear on the lips (e.g. h, s, t) and many sounds have similar lip patterns (e.g. man, pad, bat). Successful lip-reading requires a knowledge of spoken language, a knowledge of the context of the conversation, ideal conditions and a lot of guesswork.

◄ Activity 11
Watch a television news programme for 20 minutes with the sound turned off and see how much you understand.

News presenters are especially selected for their clear speech and presentation of standard English; they appear full-face in ideal light and use photographs and film footage as illustration. This is as good as it gets! ◄

'Sign language is a simple form of English produced on the hands' (Statement 9)

British Sign Language, the sign language of the British Deaf community is, in fact, not based upon English at all, but has its own distinct grammar and syntax. BSL is one of a number of natural languages that takes place in a visual–spatial medium. In common with other minority languages, such as Welsh, BSL will sometimes use the form of dominant language when referring to proper names or new terms arising out of developing technology. In these instances BSL users will finger spell the English word. Once a sign is developed for the name or the new term, finger spelling becomes unnecessary.

The struggle for the language is central to the history of the Deaf community. And the active suppression of BSL for more than 100 years through a policy of oral education for deaf children has been a major threat to the development of the Deaf community.

'Deaf people are prevented from adopting children' (Statement 16)

There is no law against deaf people adopting a child; in practice, however, it becomes extremely difficult. There is little real access for deaf people either to local authority or to voluntary adoption agencies. Publicity is not targeted at the Deaf community and information is not provided in a way that deaf people can easily understand. For example, it is not uncommon for deaf people to be interviewed by an adoption agency worker who cannot communicate with them and without the assistance of an appropriate interpreter. The approval process for prospective adopters is long and complicated and little allowance is made for deaf applicants.

Society is inclined to want to 'normalize' deaf children, which means that those deaf children who need a substitute family are likely to be placed with a hearing family who will encourage them to speak. This contrasts with the situation for Black children described in Section 3. The argument for placing a deaf child with a Deaf family to help the child develop his or her identity as a Deaf person is one that has to be constantly raised because the idea runs contrary to most current adoption practice.[4]

[4]This is discussed in B. Warr (1990) *The Deaf Child in Care*, British Agencies for Adoption and Fostering (BAAF), no.13. This argues that, for many deaf children, placement in Deaf families may well be the most appropriate. This book is not essential reading for the course, but is interesting for those concerned with these issues, and is very readable.

As you check your answers to the 'statements about deaf people', consider what may underpin each statement, and pursue the implications further than a simple answer.

Now return to Video One. This time, as you watch bear in mind the information you have gained from working on this unit. For example, pay particular attention to the way that sign language is used. Does it look like a manual form of English, or a language with its own form? And do deaf children develop appropriately or not, growing up with deaf parents? Look particularly for the quality of the communication and interaction between the different generations in the family and the level of trust and understanding demonstrated.

6.2 The rest of the course

In this unit we have introduced you to Deaf people through the video and Reader One. We have identified the group of deaf people who are the focus of the course. Through a consideration of popular stereotypes we have seen how deafness is usually portrayed as a problem, but other accounts have shown that this is not inevitable. In Block 1 you will be introduced to various aspects of the lives of Deaf people, particularly their community, culture and language. As you read these, you will find it useful to contrast the images presented in them with those presented in the newspaper articles and the advertisements you have considered in this unit. The final unit of the block introduces deaf people who, for various reasons, live outside the Deaf community.

Block 2 of the course describes deaf people in a hearing world, looking in particular at education, general health and social policy. The final block, Block 3, looks at different perspectives on deafness and you will be asked to review some of the ideas introduced in this unit. As you go through the year you will find it useful to keep notes on the different views of deafness, not only as they are presented in the course but also as they are voiced in the public arena of the media, or in private conversations. A consideration of these will contribute to your study of *Issues in Deafness*.

Suggestions for further reading

At this stage in the unit you will usually find suggestions for further reading, for those of you who wish to follow up ideas developed in the unit. However, we feel for this first unit that there is no additional further reading and that the best way to develop your ideas is to familiarize yourself with Reader One and to look at media coverage of deaf people. Thus there is no further reading suggested here.

References

ASHLEY, J. (1973) 'The silent House', in Taylor, G. and Bishop, J. (eds) (1990) *Being Deaf: The Experience of Deafness*, London, Pinter Publishers. (D251 Reader One, Article 30)

BUNTING, C. (1981) *Public Attitudes to Deafness*, London, HMSO.

CHARLES, A. and COOMBS, R. (1990) 'Growing up in care', in Taylor, G. and Bishop, J. (eds) (1990) *Being Deaf: The Experience of Deafness*, London, Pinter Publishers. (D251 Reader One, Article 24)

CRADDOCK, E. (1990) 'Life at secondary school', in Taylor, G. and Bishop, J. (eds) (1990) *Being Deaf: The Experience of Deafness*, London, Pinter Publishers. (D251 Reader One, Article 11)

DAVIES, A.C. (1983) 'Hearing disorders in the population: first phase findings of the MRC national study of hearing' in Lutman, M.E. and Haggard, M.P. (eds) *Hearing Science and Hearing Disorders*, London, Academic Press.

DHSS (DEPARTMENT OF HEALTH AND SOCIAL SECURITY) (1988) *Say It Again*, London, Social Services Inspectorate.

ELSEY, S. (1990) 'Training to teach', in Taylor, G. and Bishop, J. (eds) (1990) *Being Deaf: The Experience of Deafness*, London, Pinter Publishers. (D251 Reader One, Article 14)

FINKELSTEIN, V. (1981) 'To deny or not to deny disabilities', in Brechin, A., Liddiard, P. and Swain, J. (eds) *Handicap in a Social World*, Sevenoaks, Hodder and Stoughton.

FLETCHER, L. (1987) 'Deafness: the treatment', in Taylor, G. and Bishop, J. (eds) (1990) *Being Deaf: The Experience of Deafness*, London, Pinter Publishers. (D251 Reader One, Article 7)

GOODWILL, J. (1990) 'Janet's diary', in Taylor, G. and Bishop, J. (eds) (1990) *Being Deaf: The Experience of Deafness*, London, Pinter Publishers. (D251 Reader One, Article 1)

GROCE, N.E. (1985) *Everyone Here Spoke Sign Language,* London, Harvard University Press.

JONES, L. AND PULLEN, G. (1987) *Deaf People in Europe: What They Think*, Paper presented to the X World Congress of the World Federation of the Deaf, Finland, 1987, and published in the Proceedings of that Congress (Kuurojen Liitto r.g., The Finnish Association of the Deaf).

MACDONALD, H. (1989) 'The chance to speak for ourselves', in Taylor, G. and Bishop, J. (eds) (1990) *Being Deaf: The Experience of Deafness*, London, Pinter Publishers. (D251 Reader One, Article 6)

MARKOWICZ, H. and WOODWARD, J. (1978) 'Language and the maintenance of ethnic boundaries in the deaf community', *Communication and Cognition, 2.*

MASON, C. (1990) 'School experiences', in Taylor, G. and Bishop, J. (eds) (1990) *Being Deaf: The Experience of Deafness*, London, Pinter Publishers. (D251 Reader One, Article 9)

MURPHY, P. (1990) 'How I live with deaf-blindness', in Taylor, G. and Bishop, J. (eds) (1990) *Being Deaf: The Experience of Deafness*, London, Pinter Publishers. (D251 Reader One, Article 22)

NYMAN, D. (1990) 'A deaf-gay man', in Taylor, G. and Bishop, J. (eds) (1990) *Being Deaf: The Experience of Deafness*, London, Pinter Publishers. (D251 Reader One, Article 23)

PADDEN, C. AND HUMPHRIES, T. (1988) *Deaf in America: Voices from a Culture*, London, Harvard University Press.

REID, C. (1990) 'Education for life?', in Taylor, G. and Bishop, J. (eds) (1990) *Being Deaf: The Experience of Deafness*, London, Pinter Publishers. (D251 Reader One, Article 13)

SCOTT-PARKER, S. (1989) *They Aren't in the Brief*, London, Kings Fund Centre.

TAYLOR, G. and BISHOP, J. (eds) (1990) *Being Deaf: The Experience of Deafness*, London, Pinter Publishers. (D251 Reader One)

WOODWARD, J. (1972) 'Implication for sociolinguistic research among the deaf', *Sign Language Studies*, 1.

WOOLLEY, M. (1987) 'Acquired hearing loss: acquired oppression', in Taylor, G. and Bishop, J. (eds) (1990) *Being Deaf: The Experience of Deafness*, London, Pinter Publishers. (D251 Reader One, Article 31)

Acknowledgements

Grateful acknowledgement is made to the following sources for permission to reproduce material in this unit:

Text

Groce, N. E. (1985) *Everyone Here Spoke Sign Language: Hereditory Deafness on Martha's Vineyard*, reprinted by permission of the publishers, Harvard University Press, copyright © 1985 by Nora Ellen Groce; Padden, C. and Humphries, T. (1988) *Deaf in America: Voices From a Culture*, reprinted by permission of the publishers, Harvard University Press, copyright © 1988 by the President and Fellows of Harvard College; Etherington, S. 'Letter and Editor's Note', *Community Care*, 1 September 1988, reproduced by permission of Stuart Etherington and Read Business Publishing Group.

Newspaper excerpts

Excerpt 1 courtesy of the Peterborough Evening Telegraph Company Limited; *Excerpt 2* courtesy of the *Derby Evening Telegraph*; *Excerpt 3* courtesy of the *Evening Standard*; *Excerpt 4* courtesy of Hull and Grimsby Newspapers; *Excerpt 5* courtesy of the *Southern Evening Echo*; *Excerpt 6* courtesy of the *Dewsbury Reporter*; *Excerpt 7* courtesy of the *Doncaster Star*; *Excerpt 8* courtesy of the *Dunstable Gazette*; *Excerpt 9* courtesy of the *Bolton Evening News*; *Excerpt 10* courtesy of the *Daily Express*; *Excerpt 11* courtesy of the *Bridgwater Mercury*; *Excerpt 12* courtesy of *Therapy Weekly*; *Excerpt 13* courtesy of Rosie Barnes and *Mail on Sunday*.

Figures

Figure 1.2 courtesy of Sandra Smith; *Figures 1.10, 1.11, 1.12, 1.13, 1.14, 1.15* The Royal National Institute for the Deaf; *Figures 1.16, 1.17, 1.18* The Royal Association in Aid of Deaf People.

Grateful acknowledgement is made to Trevor Landell for permission to use his painting on the covers and title pages throughout the units of this course.

Appendix

Excerpt 1

A young couple have married in a local village church—with the ceremony interpreted by sign language experts.

For Nichola Davies and Peter Nicholson are both deaf and interpreters from Sheffield were there to translate for the couple and dozens of guests from clubs for the deaf.

Now the newly-weds are honeymooning in the glamorous Caribbean ... after speaking their own vows in Ketton parish church, and proving that love conquers all.

And there were tears of joy as the happy pair exchanged vows—something they were determined to do in spite of their handicap.

The bride's mother, Mrs Jane Davies, who runs the village post office, said: "Everyone was crying tears of joy. Even the vicar said he had a lump in his throat.

"It was a wonderful day. We were all so happy for Nichola and Peter. Now they are looking forward to a new life in Sheffield."

The couple met more than two years ago when they were on holiday in Israel with the Deaf Christian Fellowship. Romance blossomed as Nichola, deaf from birth through German measles, returned to her work as a machinist at Corah in Oakham.

Peter, like Nichola, struggled to lead a normal life in spite of his handicap. He is a clerical assistant in Sheffield Town Hall.

The couple will make their home there after their honeymoon in St Lucia.

(From the Peterborough Evening Telegraph, 29 June 1989)

Excerpt 2

A love beyond words

Loving couple Sarah Stone and Stuart Dixon are all set to say "I Do"—in sign language. For two vicars will be on hand at their wedding on Saturday to make sure the ceremony goes smoothly.

Sarah and Stuart have both been locked in a world of silence since birth after they were born profoundly deaf.

Wedding

But on Saturday two vicars will be on hand to help them through their big day—Sinfin St Stephens Rev Martin White, as well as the city's chaplain to the deaf Jean Semeonoff.

Mr White will be conducting his last wedding at the Sinfin Lane church. And Mrs Semeonoff will make a special trip to let the couple take their vows using sign language.

Teenager Sarah (19), a head cook at Kedleston Hall, met her fiance Stuart (33), of Granville Avenue, Long Eaton, 18 months ago at Derby's Rycote Centre for the deaf.

Sarah's proud mum Val Stone (35) of Montrose Close, Sinfin, said: "They're absolutely delighted about the special arrangements—the ceremony would have been really difficult for them without Mrs Semeonoff's help."

Mother-of-four Mrs Stone added: "We'll be practising tomorrow night just to make sure everything is all right for Saturday."

(From the Derby Evening Telegraph, 20 July 1988)

Excerpt 3

Parents who will never hear their baby cry

Newborn baby Charlotte Taylor cries as she poses for a photograph—but parents Mark and Elizabeth are oblivious to her yells.

For this is no ordinary family snap. The loving couple will never hear their baby's cries nor her first words—both are totally deaf.

Mark and Elizabeth, who were both born deaf, became childhood sweethearts after meeting at the Sir Winston Churchill School for the Deaf at Woodford.

Excellent

The devoted couple from Thundersley, Essex, who have never heard each other say: "I love you," married three years ago at St Andrew's Church, Rochford, Essex.

They have fought to overcome their handicap and now are adapting to the role of bringing up a baby.

Mark's mother, Mrs June Taylor, said: "They are overjoyed by the birth of Charlotte. But of course they have had to make special plans that a couple with hearing would not have to make."

A vibrator pad under their pillow is connected to a microphone in the baby's cot to alert them if Charlotte cries in the night.

A system of light bulbs around the house connected to the microphone warn them at other times.

Aircraft spares worker Mark, 24, said: "The system works very well. We are enjoying being parents. We would like one more child eventually."

Both Mark and Elizabeth have limited speech, and communicate mainly by lip-reading and writing. They decided to call the baby Charlotte because although not their first choice, they found they were able to pronounce the name without too much difficulty.

Mark's father, engineer Brian Taylor, 49, said: "They will make fabulous parents. The whole family will rally round so that we can all help with any difficulties that might arise in teaching Charlotte to speak, read and write."

Excerpt 4

Understanding on both sides

At first sight there does not seem to be anything extraordinary about the couple who live at ... Beverley. Chris spent several years working as a laboratory technician before gaining an honours degree in psychology from Hull University and Julliette trained as a secretary before she became a housewife and mother to two children.

They appear to live normal lives, yet Chris is profoundly deaf and his wife is partially deaf.

Chris chatted to me about the problem of deafness—the first I realised immediately—communication. I had to sit in a chair with the light on my face and speak slowly and clearly so that Chris could read my lips, while he had to speak slowly too so that I could work out what he said from the slightly stilted and distorted speech.

Specialising with the deaf in his degree, Chris won the class prize and will be going on to research into computer aided instruction for the deaf next year.

He told me about the difficulties he had when studying. "Lectures were impossible for me as I could not get near enough to see the lecturers lips moving while seminars posed a different problem. When you are in a group and someone stops speaking, you do not know where to look to see who is speaking next."

Used books

The education authority were unable to provide Chris with an interpreter. "They could not afford it so I did most of my work from books," said Chris.

Chris's achievements in gaining a degree is (*sic*) often held up to parents as an example of what a deaf person can do but Chris admits he was fortunate. "I was an only child and my mother spend (*sic*) many hours teaching me how to lip read and speak before I went to school.

"Later I was fortunate enough to be selected for the only Grammar School for the deaf in the country."

The Mary Hare Grammar School opened in 1946 in Newbury, Berkshire, and takes 40 pupils each year out of around 700 applicants.

Not sure

"Educationally I was lucky and I was also fortunate to have few of the social problems which many deaf people develop, mainly due to an inability to communicate between them and their parents.

"They must learn to live with their handicap and also realise that in many cases it will hinder their choice of career. It must also be faced that few deaf people will have the opportunity to achieve a degree.

"In these days when a telephone is important in most positions of responsibility when fast communications is (*sic*) necessary, the person who is unable to use it will be by-passed for promotion."

This has happened to both Chris and Julliette in their careers and Chris is not sure what he will do after his research is complete.

Way forward

"I would like to teach but because I am deaf I cannot, similarly Julliette's job as a secretary was hampered when she could not deal with clients over the phone.

"Modern communications are helping the deaf too so we cannot complain—with teletext we have information at our finger tips and are now able to understand television programmes."

"The way forward as I see it is for more understanding on both sides and for deaf people to learn to live with their handicap with the acceptance of hearing people."

(From Hull and Grimsby Newspapers)

Excerpt 5

DEAF CAN NOW JOIN IN JOYS OF CAROL SINGING

Deaf people in Hampshire will not be left out of carol singing this festive season.

A special pre-Christmas service is being held at Winchester Cathedral for both deaf and hearing people.

And one of the features will be members of choirs who "sing" through the use of sign language.

The Reverend John Studd, chaplain to the regional deaf, said they helped to add to the service for deaf people.

"It is to give them as near as possible the same sort of share and participation in worship as hearing people would have.

"Choirs aren't just for hearing people."

Mr Studd will be taking the service, both speaking and using sign language.

It will also include a musical group, Lightswitch from Bursledon, to lead some of the singing, though the congregation will be expected to be in good voice, and a performance by a deaf youth club.

The service on this Sunday, starting at 6.30 pm, will be held in the presence of the Bishop of Winchester the Right Reverend Colin James.

Mr Studd said the combined service at Winchester this year replaced the usual annual church rally.

"I am hoping that this rather different format will prove a success with the deaf communities in the diocese."

Deaf singing choir members will be attending from all over the diocese, including the Southampton, Basingstoke and Poole areas.

(From the Southern Evening Echo, 8 December 1988)

Excerpt 6

BEING DEAF NEVER STOPS THEIR FUN ███

Deaf children can have as much fun as children who can hear—and they proved it at a Christmas party held at Dewsbury Deaf Centre, Oxford Road.

But one poignant thought remained. Deaf children would never be able to hear Christmas bells or sing carols like other children.

The children, 20 in all, found ways of communicating with each other.

Superintendent Officer at the centre, Mr John Parker, said "It didn't matter that some were deaf—they all had a good time.

"They don't need to use sign language when they are young. Deaf children know what is happening through facial expressions. That's why it is easy for young deaf children to communicate with hearing children."

Brothers, sisters and friends joined in with the celebrations. They played games and were visited by Father Christmas. John said the event was a huge success.

Christmas is a visual experience—children look at Father Christmas, at the grotto, at his helpers, and at lights.

"Deaf children learn to rely on their sight more than hearing children," said John.

"They tend not to take visual things for granted, and as Christmas is more visual than other festivities, they do benefit."

Holding parties for deaf and partially hearing children is a tradition that started in 1891.

The centre moved to Oxford Road 20 years ago and took the tradition with it.

This year's party was organised by John and deaf and hearing members of the management committee, and was financed by voluntary contributions.

The event gives deaf and partially deaf youngsters the chance to get together and not to feel isolated.

Deaf children are not the only ones who can feel alone.

"Parents are usually shattered when they find out their children are deaf or have hearing difficulties," said Mr Parker.

"Public awareness about deafness is limited as it is an invisible disability. The centre helps and advises parents and children and we can get them in contact with others in a similar situation through the National Deaf Children['s] Society."

Deafness is not heredity (*sic*); John's parents, Norman and Mary, are deaf but he, and his children, can hear perfectly.

"My grandparents had six children. The first, third and fifth could hear, the rest were deaf. There have been no further signs of deafness in the family."

The centre can help provide aids for deaf and partially deaf children.

Anybody who wants help, advice or a list of provisions for the deaf and partially deaf can contact John at the centre, 10 Oxford Road, Dewsbury, telephone Dewsbury 461940.

(By Christina Littlewood in the Dewsbury Reporter, 23 December 1988)

Excerpt 7

Deaf BMX whizzkid Matthew a 'wheel' wonder

Cycling whizzkid Matthew Blackburn is heading for BMX fame—even though he cannot hear the start of each race.

For Matthew, aged nine, of Fox Lane, Frecheville, Sheffield, has been deaf since birth and attends the partial-hearing unit at Greystones Middle School.

Disability
His disability does not stop him taking his place on the starting line—or from taking second place in his section at the recent annual Sheffield BMX Club presentation evening.

Concession
The only concession made to his disability is that, as the race starter shouts "Go", dad George taps Matthew's helmet to send him on his way.

"Matthew is not the star of the Sheffield BMX by a long chalk, but at least he is trying and not allowing his disability to hold him back," said Mr Blackburn.

"We would like to see more deaf children in Sheffield involved in the sport."

(By John Highfield in the Doncaster Star, 29 September 1989)

Excerpt 8

TOWN RALLIES TO AID BRAVE LOUIS

Dunstable is rallying round to raise £15,000 for a brave two-year-old boy left profoundly deaf by meningitis.

Little Louis Francis needs a cochlear implant to live as normal a life as possible and to stop his speech being affected.

"He doesn't respond to a hearing-aid set at 140 decibels," said mum Margaret Dunne. "The doctors are still checking but they have had no response so far."

(By David Tooley in the Dunstable Gazette, 24 January 1990)

Excerpt 9

A Samaritan lifeline for deaf victims

A lifeline for deaf people throughout the North has been launched at the Samaritans' Bolton branch.

The unique scheme will enable the deaf and hard of hearing to send messages on the Samaritans' 24-hour telephone service for the first time.

The 'Textphone' system was launched by actress Elizabeth Quinn, who made an inaugural call from Telecom Tower in London to Bolton Samaritans' Bark Street office.

The call was received by Linda, one of several local Samaritans who has been trained in understanding the needs and problems of deaf people.

Bolton in the North and Putney in the South were chosen to take part in the pilot scheme. If it is successful it will be extended to other Samaritan branches all over the country.

The special telephones were provided by the Royal National Institute for the Deaf and running costs will be met by the Samaritans.

A £400 cheque to help pay for the new system was presented to Bolton Samaritans' director, Geraldine, by Turton Rotary Club president, Frank Lord, at the opening ceremony.

To use the system, deaf people type out messages on their telephone keyboards. These messages appear on a screen on the Samaritans' telephone and the reply is sent and received in the same way.

(From the Bolton Evening News, 7 October 1989)

Excerpt 10

KITTEN CLUE TO 'DEAF' MURDER

Detectives believe deaf murder victim Susanne Greenhills' killer pounced on her as she put her kitten out for the night.

Susanne, 20, could not hear him creep up behind her. And because she could not speak, she could not cry for help.

"She was tragically vulnerable," Gwent CID Detective Chief Superintendent Mark Walters said yesterday.

Susanne was found knifed to death at the flat in Tewkesbury Walk, Newport by fiance Tony Wesson, 24.

Police believe the motive was sexual, but it has not been established whether Susanne was raped.

Det. Chief Supt. Walters said: "We know she would allow her cat to run among the bushes outside her home.

"She would have had to wait for it to come back and this may be when her killer struck."

Boyfriend Tony, who is also deaf, discovered Susanne's body on Friday, but police believe she may have been murdered on Wednesday.

She normally visited a relative on Wednesdays, but last week she failed to turn up.

Susanne's home lies on a short cut to a council estate and police believe her killer may have been a late night drinker on his way home.

Forensic experts are taking samples for genetic fingerprinting and yesterday one detective said: "Genetic material could be the key to the case."

Tony Wesson's mother said yesterday: "Susanne and Tony had their ups and downs, but they found comfort together and Tony is beside himself."

(By Alun Rees in the Daily Express, 4 July 1988)

Excerpt 11

Deaf Scott amazes his family and driving instructor

Scott Davey, who has been profoundly deaf since birth, amazed his family and driving instructor when he passed his driving test first time.

Scott's mother, Ann said: "We were all thrilled with his success. He was determined to pass, so he put everything into it, all his concentration."

Scott took driving lessons from Bill Taylor from Hillstart Driving School, and Ann said: "He was marvellous with him, if Scott wasn't getting something quite right he'd get in the driving seat and demonstrate, so Scott could see how it was done. Mostly the instructions were written down or he used hand signals.

"Deafness is a very lonely handicap, but because he has been deaf since birth Scott was determined to prove that it doesn't make any difference. He seems to have a gift for driving. Being deaf does not mean you are daft.

"Driving will open up many more doors for him. He will be able to travel to different deaf clubs, and meet other deaf people. He would also love to belong to a Carnival club, and that would mean he could join in activities with hearing people, as well as giving him the chance to meet with a wider social circle. Driving is the answer to a lot of his problems.

"It was a bit of an anti-climax after he had passed because he doesn't have a car, but that will be something for him to save for."

In June Scott leaves the college in Exeter for the deaf and will have to find a job. His mother said: "He would love to have a driving job, he's very keen. That will be the next hurdle."

But the next aim for Scott is to own his own car, so until he can save up enough money he tries to win a car by entering all the competitions he can find which offer a car as the first prize.

(By Michelle French in the Bridgwater Mercury, Taunton, 6 February 1990)

Excerpt 12

DEAF SCHOOLCHILDREN 'FACE RISK OF SEXUAL ABUSE'

Transport arrangements for deaf schoolchildren are leaving them open to the risk of sexual abuse, says the National Deaf Children's Society.

In a report which claims widespread concern by parents for their children's safety when travelling to school, the NDCS has called for urgent changes to be introduced.

The society wants children to be accompanied by escorts who have been properly vetted and are employed by the education authority.

The report says: "With the rise in public awareness of child abuse, it is understandable that the parents of deaf children may feel their children to be more at risk, especially in the presence of adults whom they do not know and who are not employees of the education authority."

Government guidelines on the protection of children say people with "substantial opportunity of access to children" should be vetted. But this does not cover drivers.

Harry Cayton, NDCS director, said: "We are not saying that taxi drivers are more likely to abuse children than anybody else." But drivers taking one or two children home, without an escort, the report points out, "are often working in circumstances which the same circular says should lead to a person being subjected to checks."

Apart from the risk of abuse, parents are concerned that not all cars have rear seatbelts and that pick-up times can mean children are left waiting alone in the play-ground.

Sandra Arrowsmith, Scarborough, has been campaigning to improve the travel arrangements for her nine-year-old daughter Charlotte.

Mrs Arrowsmith complained to the NDCS that the education authority "seem to have an expectation that the parents of special needs children are prepared to take risks with their children other parents would not take."

Among the society's recommendations are that education authorities should publish their transport policies; that if the authority does not provide its own transport, only licenced taxi firms be used, and that front and rear seatbelts be provided and worn.

(From Therapy Weekly, 7 September 1989)

Excerpt 13

Why I would have an abortion

Last Friday in the Commons I voted against David Alton's abortion bill.

I did so as a woman, as a mother, as someone who cares—I believe in life every bit as much as those who collect together under the banner of the Pro-Life lobby.

But most of all, I did so as a woman who has twice had to go through that appalling personal anguish of deciding whether or not I ought to have an abortion.

Many people today believe abortions only happen to the young and irresponsible, the kind of woman who takes risks and sleeps around.

But if David Alton's bill, lowering the limits of abortion from 28 to 18 weeks, goes through, many mothers just like me—with happy families like mine—will suffer.

Most abortions are done well before 18 weeks, only 5 per cent are late. Last year only 29 were performed between 24 and 28 weeks. Those late abortions would have been heart-rending decisions, made in exceptional circumstances.

Late abortions occur because tests can only be done at 16 weeks and results come through at 20 weeks; they occur because very young girls are frightened to say they are pregnant; they occur because the victims of sexual abuse often conceal such things.

My personal nightmare began when I was 26. It was my first pregnancy, and I did a brief spell of teaching at a Greenwich school. A lively little boy called William was unusually mopey and all he wanted to do was sit on my knee all day. A few days later, his mother told me he'd got German measles.

I hadn't been vaccinated, and very soon I was covered in a rash. My doctor knew I was 13 weeks pregnant and told me to contact a clinic right away. When I got there they tried to make out I had an 'hysterical rash'. But they did tests and it took seven weeks for the results to come through.

Even then I had to make an appointment to be told what I already knew, that I had had German measles and that my baby might be born handicapped.

By that time, through no fault of my own, an abortion would have been a properly induced labour. Doctors told me there was a 10 per cent chance of handicap, and were specific that it would probably be hearing and co-ordination.

They told me this on a Friday. If I wanted the abortion I had to go for it on the Sunday. They gave me 24 hours to decide. Graham, my husband, and I sat up all night. I already felt very attached to the baby. 1 wanted that baby, not any other. We were both very idealistic, and I just didn't know what I was letting myself and my baby in for.

At 5 am I decided to go ahead and have the baby, it was an agonising decision. Because of what I know now, it was the right decision—but only just. My son Daniel, who has only partial hearing, was subject to tormenting jibes because of his hearing aid as soon as he started school.

They called him Daniel Deafo. At night he often cried, and was afraid of going to school.

One of his teachers says she thinks he will be a happier adult. He hasn't had a happy childhood, and his handicap is only mild. But what if I had caught the Rubella virus a week or two earlier, and he'd been born blind and dumb as well? I would definitely have had a termination. I am no longer idealistic.

One woman from Pro-Life, with a fertility problem, asked if I would have had an abortion knowing there were people who were prepared to adopt a severely handicapped child. I said yes. She said I was 'sick'.

I was furious. I've had three children, and it is for me, as their mother, to make the decision, not for my convenience, but in the child's long term interest.

Thirteen years after Danny, I was faced with the same horrible situation again. Pregnant again at 39, I had to have a test. The chance of handicap goes up the older you get. But the test could not be confirmed until I was at 20 weeks.

At Christmas, 1984, I went to a school fete, and saw a large Downs Syndrome man being helped by his mother, a frail old lady.

Knowing how Danny had suffered, I wondered what kind of life that person had had? What would life be like in the future for him, and the rest of his family?

I went home and wept. I knew then I would have a termination if they found my baby was handicapped. But the test was clear, and Joseph was a fine healthy baby. Let's be brutally clear, there is a social issue that every woman has to consider.

My other children were 12 and nine, and would it have been fair to them to have a handicapped child which would need all my attention? When I was a girl I knew a woman who had a Downs baby late in life, the thought of what he would do when she was gone haunted her so badly that she committed suicide. The boy went into an institution and her teenage daughter was left alone.

Handicapped children do not [always] lead rich, full lives in this country. They do not [always] bring blessings to their families. The rate of divorce is higher in such families. Above all, there is the attitude of society to handicapped people which is to patronise and belittle them.

Life, you see, is for living not just existing. I believe.

(By Rosie Barnes in the Mail on Sunday, 24 January 1988)